629.225   Rogers, Hal.
ROG
          Tow trucks.

$21.36

Rescue Machines At Work

Tow Trucks

By Hal Rogers

The Child's World® Inc. ◆ Eden Prairie, Minnesota

Published by The Child's World®, Inc.
7081 W. 192 Ave.
Eden Prairie, MN 55346

Design and Production:
The Creative Spark, San Juan Capistrano, CA

Photos: © 1998 David M. Budd Photography

Library of Congress Cataloging-in-Publication Data

Rogers, Hal, 1966-
      Tow trucks / by Hal Rogers.
         p. cm.
      Includes index.
      Summary: Describes the parts of a tow truck, how to operate them,
and the work they do.
      ISBN 1-56766-658-2 (lib. bdg. : alk. paper)
      1. Wreckers (Vehicles)—Juvenile literature. [1. Wreckers.
(Vehicles)] I. Title.
   TL230.5.W74R64 1999
   629.225—dc21
                                                             99-28597
                                                             CIP

Contents

On the Job

On the job, tow trucks **tow** cars and trucks that do not work. A tow truck takes a broken truck to get **repaired.**

The tow truck has a long, metal arm.

The worker attaches the arm to

the truck.

The tow truck has many **bins.** The worker

stores tools in the bins.

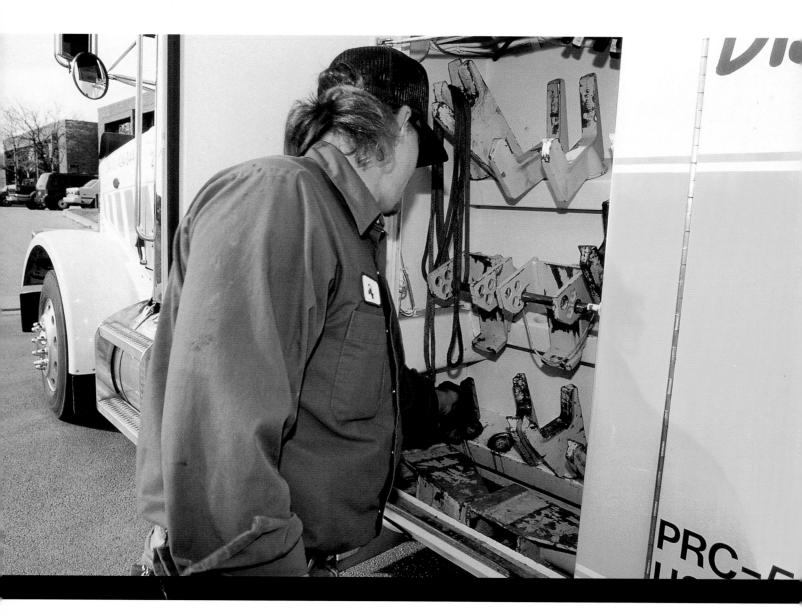

The worker uses **levers** to make the arm work. They are also inside of a bin. The tow truck's arm reaches under the truck.

The arm is very strong. It can even lift

a giant truck off the ground!

The tow truck pulls the truck to a **garage.** Chains keep the truck attached to the arm when the tow truck moves.

Sometimes even a fire engine doesn't work. The tow truck can tow a fire engine to the garage, too.

16

The tow truck has another arm called a **boom.** It moves up and down. What if a car slides into a ditch? Then it cannot drive out by itself. The worker attaches the boom to the car. The tow truck can lift it out of the ditch.

Climb Aboard!

Would you like to see where the driver sits?

The driver is called an **operator.** He sits inside

the **cab. Controls** help him drive the truck.

The operator has a special **radio.** He uses it to

talk to a **dispatcher.** The dispatcher tells the

operator where he needs to go.

Up Close

The inside

1. The radio

2. The steering wheel

3. The controls

The outside

1. The arm

2. The cab

3. The boom

4. The tool bins

23

Glossary

bins (BINZ)
Bins are boxes inside the tow truck. The worker stores tools inside the bins.

boom (BOOM)
The boom is a long arm on the tow truck. The worker attaches the boom to the cars and trucks it tows.

cab (KAB)
A cab is the place where the tow truck's driver sits. The cab has a seat, a steering wheel, controls, and a radio.

controls (kun-TROLZ)
Controls are tools used to help make something work. The operator uses controls to make a tow truck work.

dispatcher (dis-PACH-ur)
A dispatcher is a person who works with the tow truck's operator. The dispatcher tells the operator where he or she needs to go.

garage (guh-RAJ)
A garage is a place that repairs cars and trucks. Tow trucks sometimes take other cars and trucks to a garage.

levers (LEV-erz)
The tow truck's levers are metal bars with black knobs at the end. The operator uses levers to move the tow truck's arm.

operator (OPP-er-ay-ter)
The operator is the person who drives the tow truck. He or she also works the arm and the boom.

radio (RAYD-ee-o)
A radio is a special machine on a tow truck. The operator uses the radio to talk to the dispatcher.

repaired (ree-PAYRD)
If people repair something, they fix it. Workers at a garage repair cars and trucks.

tow (TOW)
When a tow truck tows a car or truck, it pulls it along behind it. A tow truck tows cars and trucks that do not work.